Sex in the Kingdom

Sexual Strongholds and Kingdom Principles

Apostle Stanley J. Alexander

Publisher bylisabell
Radical Women
(DBA)
PO Box 782
Granbury, TX
76048
www.bylisabell.com

ISBN: **978-1-7340398-0-1**

DEDICATION

To all believers, unlock at personal risk!

"Therefore; to him who knows to do good and does not
do it, to him it is sin."

James 4:17

Contents

Acknowledgements

In life, one might have the chance to hold something priceless such as a rare gem, diamond, or any type of valuable possession. One might have a chance to come across something so beautiful it's breathtaking. One might even have a chance to experience something that brings them absolute joy for one moment. However, I can justly say I have all of this and more in one woman—my wife. In life, never overlook what you have for what you are trying to get. I truly thank the love of my life, Paula Alexander, for being who she is to our family, and that's truly a blessing.

To my "5 P's" (Porsche, Portia, Porshawn, Porshanna, and Porshalyn), each of you have given me a purpose to press forward when times were hard. Otherwise, I possibly would have given up a long time ago.
To the *Surge Center*, I offer and receive much love.
To all my family and friends, I love you all dearly.
Special thanks to Elizabeth H. Hicks for her editing skills and helping me bring the words of the Father to life. To Lisa Bell of Radical Women, thank you for the final edits, formatting and developing this book beyond my capabilities to make it the best possible and publishing the final work.

~Introduction~

The Kingdom of God has so many teachings on various topics. Some of those topics are easy to accept, while other topics have to grow on us over time or from the in-depth study. I truly believe this book requires studying. When read alone, these words may never grow on us. Identifying biblical strongholds previously accepted by many is challenging. But when approached, they challenge our inner spirit. This leads to spiritual warfare and affects our spirit either knowingly or unknowingly, leading us to deliverance or defeat. One of these strongholds is sex in the Kingdom.

Sex in the Kingdom of God is a topic upon which many tread lightly. Many see it as a beehive they do not want to stir up because, without proper knowledge and guidance, the subject can become dangerous—like disturbing a hive of bees.

There are many truths written in this book concerning the act of sex in the Kingdom of God. However, many will not dare open it for fear of conviction by God's truth. Reading and studying this subject becomes risky. For when we know the truth, we can no longer escape the consequences of disobedience. We no longer have the ability to justify behavior or excuse it if we know the truth. And we can no longer say, "I didn't know better."

Nevertheless, I dare you to continue reading. Take that risk. To do anything less leaves you open to a less-fulfilling life and at a greater risk—missing the fullness of God through obedience and understanding of what He intends.

Sex in the Kingdom isn't something to avoid. God created sex, and contrary to some beliefs, sex was not the original sin. The world and Satan made sex something less than the gift God intended. When we view, understand and practice sex as He meant, we get to relish this wonderful gift.

So, keep reading and discover more about this topic. You won't regret it.

~Knowing the Author~

Stanley James Alexander was born in Dallas, Texas to the parents of Randell Tucker and Beverly Kay Alexander. Raised most of his life in the inner city, they lived in a place known to many as South Dallas. He grew up in BONTON projects and Rose Terrace projects. With his mother in a single-parent home, he survived as part of a family consisting of six siblings. Four boys, Randell T. Tucker Jr., Curtis Alexander, Charles Alexander, and Stanley, plus two girls, Cassandra Alexander and Lonette Alexander.

"My mother raised all of us to know who our Lord and Savior was, and we were all given a choice of how life would be for each of us," he shared.

The life he elected landed him in San Pablo, California. He was blessed with an environment of what society labels as a healthy family—his Uncle Val Jean Daniels (a father figure) and Aunt Patricia A. Daniels (a mother figure). He is indebted to her for the countless days and nights staying up studying. To my number one cousin, Brett Daniels, much love.

The Bible says, "Know those that labor among you." (1Thessalonians 5:12) Surrounded by an immense amount of information and literature readily available, much comes in the form of dogmatic writing ideas or principles unproven or unexamined. If one studies the author before studying the information or literature, one may know where the writer aims his or her focus. Truths from the Bible are just that, but in our God-given ability to choose, many find themselves holding on to the dogma rather than truth.

It is critical to take out time to study the author before studying anything written. Stanley bases his writing on the truth found in the Bible. Thus, it cannot be placed on the list of dogmatic writing due to the truth openly expressed throughout the reading of this book. He will repeat some of this information when the Lord allows him to write a book of his testimony. Until then, may the Lord lead you to the truth about *Sex in the Kingdom*.

Chapter 1
~Getting the Mind Ready~

"Therefore; to him who knows to do good and does not do it, to him it is sin."
(James 4:17, NKJV)

To enter this, or any, spiritual journey, each person must take out time to be spiritually lead and not driven by the course our flesh takes us.

Quite some time ago, the Holy Spirit led me to a book, which many in the body of Christ also find indispensable.

The *Little Red Prayer Book*.[1] continues as an excellent resource for all of my life and for that of others. If you haven't heard of it or enjoyed a

[1] (Richard Broadbent 2012)

chance to use it, visit www.christianword.org for a free copy. The Bible says let every person work under, or by, the oracles God provided them and prayer. (1Peter 4:11) I find this book helps me with my prayer life.

For the spiritual journey contained through *Sex in the Kingdom*, I strongly encourage every reader to prepare with prayer. I listed a few prayers below to get the reader's mind, heart, and spirit in the right place to receive what I feel the Spirit wants to say to the Body of Christ. However, I want the reader to listen as much to Him as to my words, and the best way to accomplish that task comes with prayer

"Remove Any Deception"

Heavenly Father, I (we) come to you through the precious Blood of my (our) Lord and Savior Jesus Christ. I (we) ask You to destroy and remove any deception in my (our) minds. In Jesus Christ's Holy Name, Amen.

This journey represents a hard place for many as we engage in Spiritual Warfare. The enemy longs for us to remain deceived, and when we seek truth, he uses tactics to keep us from learning God's truth. The Bible tells us not to believe every spirit, so this prayer asks Him to guide us spiritually to His truth.

"Testing the Spirits"

Heavenly Father, it is written in Your Word in 1 John 4:1-2 that we should not believe every spirit, but test the spirits to determine whether the spirits are of God. By this, I will know the spirit of God: for every spirit that confesses that Jesus Christ has come in the flesh is of God. Heavenly Father, if you told me to confess, "Jesus Christ has come in the flesh." Amen.

I do believe Jesus came in the flesh, and I proclaim that the same Spirit blessed me to write this book.

For many years, the types of sex mentioned in this book were not common among many people. Only a few admitted they partook in these sexual acts. Now they openly exist in many of the body of Christ's households. People never know something has a grip on them until they have to do without it. Now we must face spiritual strongholds and readily confess they reside in us.

Shattering Strongholds on Self

Heavenly Father, I come to You now in the Name of my Lord and Savior Christ Jesus. Heavenly Father, I am standing on the truth of your Word. You said you would give me the keys to the Kingdom, that whatsoever I would bind on earth would be bound in heaven and whatsoever I would loose on earth would be loosed in heaven according to Matthew16 and 18. Right now, in the Name of Jesus Christ, I bind my will to the Will of God, that I will be constantly aware of your Will and purpose for my life. I bind myself to the truth of God that I will not be deceived by the many subtle deceptions of the world and the devil. In the Name of Jesus Christ, I bind myself to the Blood of Jesus. I want to be constantly aware of the Blood of Christ Jesus' "miracle-working power to restore and heal and keep me safe...." I repent of every wrong desire, attitude and pattern of thinking I have had. Forgive me, Heavenly Father, for holding onto wrong ideas, desires, behaviors and habits according to 1 John 1:19 and John14:14. I renounce and reject these things in the Name of the Lord Jesus Christ, and I loose every wrong attitude, pattern of thinking, belief, idea, desire, behavior and habit I have ever learned. I loose the strongholds around them that would keep me from being completely surrendered to the Will of God for my life. I loose all doubt and confusion from myself. I have bound my mind to the mind of Christ and I loose every wrong thought and evil imagination that will keep me from being in sweet unity with You. I bind and loose these things in the Name of Jesus Christ who has given me the keys to do so. Amen.

There are other prayers I could add to this book, but for space and copyright considerations, I include only these three. I encourage you to download or send for your own *Little Red Prayer Book*. I thank God for Christian Word Ministries and their willingness for others to use their prayer material. I pray that your mind is ready to encounter God's truth concerning the body of

Christ.

Now, I welcome you to *Sex in the Kingdom*.

Chapter 2
~Let's Talk About Sex~

"Therefore; to him who knows to do good and does not do it, to him it is sin."

(James 4:17, NKJV)

The Kingdom's perspective versus the world's viewpoint on sex differs significantly.

The Kingdom's version began almost from the beginning of time on earth. We see the first mention of sex in the book of Genesis, chapter 4. (KJV) "And Adam knew Eve his wife; and she conceived, and bare Cain, and said, I have gotten a man from the Lord."

The word "knew" is used to state that a place of obedience and intimacy took place at the same time. Obedience in what the Lord said in Genesis. "And God blessed them, and God said unto them,

Be fruitful and multiply, and replenish the earth." (Genesis 1:28)

When we look closer, however, we see God instituting sex before the fall of humanity. God made man and woman in His image and placed them in the garden. He fully intended for them to rule over the earth, and part of that commandment included filling it with their offspring. According to the first chapter in Genesis, God made the statement at the time of creation. Now, God didn't tell Adam and Eve how to fill the earth. He didn't go into detail about sex, but when the Lord said, "Be fruitful," the word He used meant literally to bear fruit. The word for multiply meant to be or become many. In essence, God faced the first humans and said, "Go make many more humans."

We don't know how long Adam and Eve remained in the garden before falling to Satan's deception. Nor do we know if they enjoyed sex before the fall. Perhaps they did. We do know that later, after the fall and their eviction from Eden, intimacy took place—proved by Eve's conception of a son. Her declaration of him being from the Lord further confirms that the two of them understood God's intention for their sexual relationship. God gave sex to mankind for use between husband and wife to fulfill God's master plan.

As we look at God's very first commandment

recorded, it has to do with procreation – be fruitful and multiply. This commandment came even before the instruction to subdue and rule over the earth. Don't you think if God said it first, He considered it the most important part of His plan?

The Bible demonstrates no shame when talking about sex, but the body of Christ (also known as its members) does. Somewhere along the way, we came to believe talking about sex belongs anywhere but in church. Not so with God. A poetic book in the Bible, Song of Solomon, includes scripture detailing a romantic relationship with deep words of intimacy and no shame.

Unfortunately, when put in the hands of man, sex can and will get off track. Any good thing from God placed in the hands of man can, and often does, go wrong somewhere.

Consider Adam and Eve in Eden. God placed the couple in a beautiful garden. Filled with every imaginable tree and plant, these first people had free reign to choose anything they wanted to eat. Nothing except the tree of the knowledge of good and evil was off-limits to them. Picture every fruit and vegetable you like. Adam and Eve had that vast choice, yet the one tree—the only forbidden tree—became the very one the devil used against them.

The enemy approached Eve first. She knew better than to eat from that one tree. But oh, that fruit looked so tasty. Instead of trusting God and obeying Him, she took a bite. And Adam, standing there with her, watched. Being a good wife, she shared, and the Bible doesn't say he hesitated for even a moment. He took the fruit, disregarded the one thing God said don't do, and he ate it too.

Up until that moment, we assume Adam and Eve walked in full obedience to God's commandments. With one bite, they disobeyed. As a result, Adam committed high treason.

Harsh—but true.

Genesis 2:17 states, "But of the tree of the knowledge of good and evil, thou shalt not eat of it: for in the day that thou eatest thereof thou shalt surely die."

Adam disobeyed a direct word from God, his sovereign leader, known to man as high treason. Merriam-Webster defines treason as 1: the offense of attempting by overt acts to overthrow the government of the state to which the offender owes allegiance or to kill or personally injure the sovereign or the sovereign's family

2: the betrayal of a trust: TREACHERY

The only power or overseer was God—not a country, but the Kingdom of God.

Some might say Adam didn't intentionally, commit treason against God. He didn't want to overthrow his Maker. He only wanted to keep Eve happy, and frankly, the fruit looked yummy.

While true, Adam and Eve joined with Satan in turning from God's direct command. Intentional or not, they did indeed willingly participate in the act of treason.

The fall of man caused sin to enter into their hearts, and sex took a turn for the worse. What God intended as pure and part of worship became something unholy over time. You see, sin at the core comes from humans wanting their way instead of God's plan and direction. Therefore, because of sin, we look at sex from a perspective of what we want from it, not necessarily His original intentions.

The self-centered perspective comes from men turning their ear from the Law of God, and Proverbs 28:9 states, "One who turns away his ear from hearing the law, even his prayer is an abomination." (NKJV)

Leviticus 18:1-26 gives details about how God delights when mankind uses intimacy in the way He commanded us to do so. The Old Testament provided the law on sexual immorality. The New Testament translation of sexual immorality in the Greek is porneia—also translated as whoredom, fornication and idolatry. Have you ever considered sexual sin as idolatry?

1Corinthians 6:18 puts us on high alert when it comes to sexual immorality. This scripture states to flee fornication. "Every sin that a man doeth is without the body: but he that committeth fornication sinneth against his own body."

Lying comes out of the body, killing is sometimes issued with the hands, but sexual sin incorporates the entire body to carry out the act. Although hands can be used to kill, sex involves all of the man's or woman's body parts. God gave us these to use between husband and wife. Any time we use these parts with someone to whom we are not married, we create sexual sin. When we use our body to commit these acts, we are in direct violation of 1Corinthians 6:19 which states "What? Know ye not that your body is the temple of the Holy Ghost which is in you, which ye have of God, and ye are not your own?"

This book is not written to judge the world, but to serve as a reminder to the body of Christ. It is not written to condemn but to open our eyes to a spirit that has slipped into the beds of many godly homes.

I will totally expose this spirit in the chapter, "The Study of The Matter," but first I ask that you enter this book with prayer. Next, I ask that you not have tunnel vision and see only what you want to see. Finally, I ask that you pray for and maintain a teachable spirit.

In life, when things go wrong, one must take the time to trace back to the root of the problem and find a cause. The Bible teaches us to study the

Word of God, but very few do—perhaps not knowing how or where to start. Sex in the Kingdom of God has gone too far. Too far with compromising, too far with rationalizing, too far with pretending we've done nothing wrong.

Still, when we do things our way, God has a way of getting us back on the right track. Most likely, we won't think the same way God does, but if we keep viewing and participating in sex our way, Romans 1:24 says, "Wherefore God also gave them up to uncleanness through the lusts of their own hearts, to dishonor their own bodies between themselves:"

Paul referred to Romans who God allowed to do things their way, and natural consequences caught up with them. And many Christians today face consequences because of doing things their way.

Look at the sheer number of sexually transmitted diseases. Those who continually go their way, ignoring God's commandments run the risk of natural consequences from their behavior. If you study the laws God put into practice, it quickly becomes evident that He wanted our good. And He showed us the way to live for our benefit, not out of meanness or trying to prevent us from having fun. When we ignore His ways, we take the results in our hands.

If we are truly thoughtful and honest within

ourselves, wouldn't we rather be in God's hands rather than our own?

Paul wrote, "And likewise also the men, leaving the natural use of the woman, burned in their lust one toward another; men with men, working which is unseemly, and receiving in themselves that recompense of their error which was meet." (Romans 1:27)

Centuries ago, Paul saw men and women misusing their bodies to fulfill their lusts, completely disregarding natural tendencies. Men wanted men then too. Homosexuality isn't new. Then, as now, people decided to take their ways instead of following God's intended purpose. And Paul clearly stated the people in his time suffered from natural consequences, which didn't always mean physical effects. Paul also spoke of spiritual things, which meant those people also reaped a broken relationship with God.

Paul eluded to the overall sexual immorality of his time, not merely homosexuality. We can easily focus on one aspect, but any sin looks the same to a holy God. Any immorality harms our relationship with Him. And eventually, He will allow us to go our way and pursue the things we want, but the results never give us the life He intended for us.

As the old people of God would say, "Lord, help us today."

Chapter 3
~How Did This Come About~

"My people are destroyed for lack of knowledge: because thou has rejected knowledge, I will also reject thee, that thou shalt be no priest to me: seeing thou hast forgotten the law of thy God, I will also forget thy children."

(Hosea 4:6, KJV)

Two types of people exist in this world—the good and the bad. The saved and the unsaved is an alternate way of stating this. We have only two ways of doing things in this world—God's way and the wrong way.

God's way looks out for our best interest. He knows far more than we do, even if we don't think so.

Do you remember being a child or a teenager? Perhaps your parents handed out rules you didn't like. Even imperfect parents try to teach their children to behave well enough to live in society and stay out of trouble. True, some parents don't do this well, but work with me. God isn't an imperfect parent. While we may not see the full intent of his directions, we have to trust that He sincerely wants the very best for our lives.

When we step from beneath God's protection and disobey, life goes wrong. A car may hit a child who chooses to play in the street. In the same way, life hits us hard when we make bad choices. Disobedience doesn't make us bad people, but living in constant defiance means that we need a new attitude. God doesn't allow His children to continue living in a sinful lifestyle without consequences—no more than a good parent keeps letting a small child play in the middle of a busy street.

We live in a perverse and wicked generation. Although on this earth, that statement isn't new.

Not long after Jesus returned to Heaven, the Apostle Peter preached to the crowd. As Luke recorded in the book of Acts, Peter spent a considerable amount of time talking about the prophets, Jesus, and many things they recently experienced. Then, "And with many other words did he testify and exhort, saying, Save yourselves from this untoward generation." (Acts 2:40)

The word "untoward" used in this scriptural reference is defined as perverse or crooked. Two thousand years ago, men walked in a perverse or crooked generation not so different from today's world. God always told His people not to touch the unclean things, but humans constantly seem to disregard Him.

The Bible introduces many illustrations of unclean things.

To bring the truth of God's Word to light concerning **TRUE HOLINESS** found in Leviticus 18:22-30, I must write all of this so we can see and understand the issue at hand.

Thou shalt not lie with mankind, as with womankind: it is abomination. Neither shalt thou lie with any beast to defile thyself therewith: neither shalt any woman stand a beast to lie down thereto: it is confusion. Defile not ye yourselves in any of these things: for in all these the nations are defiled which I cast out before you... Therefore shall ye keep mine ordinance, that ye commit not any one of these abominable customs, which were committed before you, and that ye defile not yourselves therein: I am the Lord your God.

One of the truths I'm going to pull out is that

these acts were customs of other people. (The word "customs" in the book of Leviticus means appointed, manner, ordinance.) Just because other people do something doesn't make it right. God gave His people laws to keep them healthy in mind, body and spirit. Those statutes recorded in Leviticus still have what we need today to remain healthy in mind, body and spirit. That is why God tells us to "come from among them and be ye separate." (2Corinthians 6:17)

The way I got here came from having a hard place in my heart for that one sin men say they would never do. Although there are many abomination sins listed in the Bible, from lying to killing, the only abominable sin we always bring up is "homosexuality." The body of Christ has its way of being blind to some truths in the Word of God. The Word of God says, "My people are destroyed for lack of knowledge: because thou hast rejected knowledge, I will also reject thee, that thou shalt be no priest to me: seeing thou hast forgotten the law of thy God, I will also forget thy children." (Hosea 4:6)

We must understand that the book of Leviticus is the book of God's Laws. By the grace of God, I never succumbed to a homosexual lifestyle, but I justified my sins by comparing them to this one because it is an abomination to God. We can always see other people's sins, but never our own. We are quick to judge all sins the eyes can see, but most often do not have the discernment to pick up the unseen sins.

One day, out of nowhere, God hit me with a blow that caused me to remove that hard place I had for the lifestyle of a homosexual.

God said, "You are a sodomite."

Insulted, I responded, perhaps not with the best attitude. "No, I am not. And by the way, God, I have not heard of that word."

Did I actually have the guts to argue with God, not even understanding the thing He convicted me about? Yes, I did. Fortunately, God, in His patience with me, continued teaching through His Spirit. That conversation gave me insight and a desire to pursue a Study of The Matter.

Chapter 4
~The Study of the Matter~

"Study to show thyself approved unto God, a workman that needeth not to be ashamed, rightly dividing the word of truth."
(2Timothy2:15, KJV)

After picking my jaw up off the floor, I brought myself to an upright position, ready to study the word *sodomite*. But God had more to tell me first.

Numbers 23:19 came to mind. "God is not a man that he should lie; neither the son of man that he should repent."

God said, "I cannot lie!"

I knew that, but His words caused me to remember Hosea 4:6.

I said, "Yes, Lord."

His gentle voice came again. "Don't be destroyed for the lack of knowledge. Knowledge is to know, but wisdom is the application of knowledge."

I thought about that statement for a moment. Then the Lord spoke again, and I recalled Paul's letter to Timothy. "Study to shew thyself approved unto God, a workman that needeth not to be ashamed, rightly dividing the word of truth." (2Timothy 2:15)

All of those thoughts mixed in my mind, and the word sodomite again popped up. Me? A sodomite?

What do you do when God hits you with a word you never heard and don't understand for a minute? The answer is quite simple. Study.

I researched the word *sodomite*—simply put, according to Merriam-Webster, this word refers to one who engages in *sodomy*. And sodomy means anal or oral copulation (aka sex) with a member of the same or opposite sex. It also carries the idea of sex with an animal (bestiality).[2]

The origin of this word comes from the story of Sodom and Gomorrah found in Genesis chapters 18-19. We'll look at this passage more closely in a moment.

---

[2] (Merriam-Webster Incorporated 2019)

Sodomy is not merely an act of Sodomites. It involves attitude as well, but the danger comes from commonly restricting the meaning to anal sex alone, and association with nothing other than homosexuality. Nowhere does the term sodomy or sodomite indicate the sexuality of a person, although the original story contained men. By placing a box around our ideas of the true meaning, we miss the point of what God wanted me to understand.

Possibly, the word or act has not hit home. Therefore, I would like to expound on the simplicity of the word as God illustrated it to me.

God stated, "Son, you are an abomination yourself. You are operating in the same spirit as a homosexual—the spirit of a sodomite."

Now, sometimes, God ruffles our feathers to get our attention. And in this case, my feathers not only ruffled, they fluffed out all over the place. I said, "No, Lord. That's man-on-man."

Have you ever tried to argue against a truth God shared with you? He patiently corrected my blunder.

"Son, that is not true."

At that point, God walked me back to when he made people.

"And God said, 'Let us make man in our image, after our likeness; and let them have dominion'… So God created man in his own image of God created he him: male and female created he them. And God blessed them, and God said unto them, 'Be **fruitful** and **multiply**, and replenish the earth…" (Genesis 1:26-28)

Intent on listening to Holy Spirit, I immediately saw what He meant to show me. God blessed them in their union, thus creating an act of worship. But the act of husband and wife coming together also had a purpose. "Be fruitful and multiply." Life exists in the seed from both parties.

In order to teach the understanding of this matter, let's go back to Genesis 1:11 for the application of an important principle.

God said, "Let the earth bring forth grass, the herb yielding seed, and the fruit tree yielding fruit after his kind, whose seed is in itself, upon the earth: and it was so."

The seed within us produces after its own kind, just as grass seed, herb seed, and the fruit tree. Each seed has a purpose to reproduce, and they can only do this by the will of God.

Looking more closely at this principle, according to Genesis 38:8-10, it is dangerous when the seed of man is wasted.

In Old Testament times, having a son as an heir held the utmost importance for a man. If a man married and then died before fathering a son, a surviving brother was to marry the widow. When the new union produced the firstborn son, that child became heir to the deceased brother. (See Deuteronomy 25:5-6.) A strange custom in today's world where often most of us receive little or no inheritance. Unless we come from a family with a great deal of money, we don't fully grasp the critical nature of having an heir.

As we read Tamar's story, we see her first husband, Er, die because of his evil ways. So Judah, her father-in-law, made sure the second son married her.

Onan, however, didn't like the idea of producing a son that wouldn't be his heir. Maybe it had to do with receiving less money or land when Judah finally left the world. Regardless of the underlying reasoning, he preferred never having a son to producing one that took his brother's name and became an heir to Er. But God disliked Onan's selfish disobedience so much that He also took the second son's life.

"And Judah said unto Onan, Go in unto thy brother's wife, and marry her, and raise up seed to thy brother. And Onan knew that the seed should not be his; and it came to pass, when he went in unto his brother's wife, that he spilled it on the ground, lest that he should give seed to his brother. And the thing which he did displeased the Lord: wherefore he slew him also."

God uses the seed of man to replenish the earth. Any action other than this is ungodly. While

I'm not speaking out against birth control, we need to remember this critical point. Sex for the sake of our pleasure and without any intent to reproduce doesn't fall under His original plan. Do we trust God to allow conception only when He knows we are ready? Most likely not. Much of that comes from the fact that we take sex lightly and enter into the act when an unplanned pregnancy has dire consequences. Within marriage, no wrong time for a baby exists if we believe He plans the best for our lives.

Romans 1:26 says, "For this cause God gave them up unto vile affections; for even their women did change the natural use into that which is against nature:"

What is the "natural use" of which Paul speaks? The kind of sex that produces life. I am not aware of any child ever conceived from oral sex or anal sex even when done between a man and woman.

I got it. The Word of God says in several places, "When a man leaves his mother and father, he cleaves to his wife, and the two shall become one." (See Genesis 2:24, Ephesians 5:31, Mark 10:7, and Matthew 19:5.) The Word of God also speaks to this in Hebrews 13:4, "Marriage is honourable in all, and the bed undefiled: but whoremongers and adulterers God will judge."

This verse is one place where the spirit of the

sodomites hides. The marriage bed is undefiled. However, to be truthful, it can include doing things our way and not God's way. The Spirit is willing, but the flesh is weak. This spirit of the sodomite has now become part of the make-up of our everyday sexual worship.

Who are the sodomites? Let's turn back to Genesis19:1-38, which establishes the first encounter with this group of people.

If you don't know this story, God planned to destroy Sodom and Gomorrah. The Bible states that people who lived in these cities lived in such an evil way everything they did reeked of wickedness. Abraham interceded because his nephew, Lot, lived in Sodom. He asked God to find 50 righteous people there and spare the city because of them.

Abraham knew better, so he decreased the number required to save the city. Repeatedly he put out a number until he got all the way down to 10 people. Just 10 righteous people, which could have been Lot's family. Unfortunately, not even 10 people lived in these ungodly cities, so God destroyed them. But God honored Abraham's faith by sending two angels, disguised as men, to visit Lot and tell him to leave.

We join the story at verse 4-5, which illustrates their actions.

"But before they (Lot's family and the angels)

lay down, the men of the city, even the men of Sodom, compassed the house round, both old and young, all the people from every quarter: And they called unto Lot, and said unto him, 'Where are the men which came in to thee this night? Bring them out unto us, that we may know them.'"

To understand this verse fully, we must reference the Word of God, precept upon precept—line upon line. The men in this evil city wanted to "know" the visiting angels. We can compare this same word when we look back at Genesis 4:1. "And Adam knew Eve his wife; and she conceived, and bare Cain, and said, 'I have gotten a man from the Lord.'"

So when the men asked to "know them," they indicated a desire to have sex with them. Let's not be remiss in understanding that the relationship Adam and Eve enjoyed included intimacy. What these men wanted to do had nothing to do with intimacy, worship or reproduction. How quickly man perverted God's original design of sex, worshipping only himself and going against one of the first commandments God uttered to humanity.

Lot responded, "I pray you, brethren do not so wickedly. Behold now, I have two daughters which have not known man: let me, I pray you, bring them out unto you, and do ye to them as is good in your eyes."

I'm not sure Lot's offering of his daughters

sounds much better, but he certainly felt an obligation to protect the angels. And he knew the men of the city, so perhaps he trusted they wouldn't accept the offer of his daughters. The men brewed in their flesh to do this evil unto these men. We must not forget a crucial fact—these people, both the males and females, also practiced prostitution and all other sorts of wickedness. The Bible makes it clear that they adopted practices according to all the abominations of the nations the Lord drove out before the people of Israel. In the process, they lived in a manner far from what God wanted. "But the men of Sodom were wicked and sinners before the Lord exceedingly." (Genesis 13:13)

Do you recall my comment that I hid behind not being gay, but God showed me how the same spirit used me?

Man! This is mind-blowing when we discover how the enemy plays us merely from a lack of knowing God's Word! Isn't that exactly what he did with Eve? Twisting words and hiding truth, the enemy loves to warp and pervert what God said.

While using the words "homosexual" or "lesbian" to title a sodomite, those two terms alone are an understatement. We show injustice to this spirit, which hides itself under these two titles and downplays all it fully depicts.

The Word of God conveys sodomites to

spotlight on the attitude. "But the men of Sodom were wicked and sinners before the Lord exceedingly." Sodomy hides itself in the beds of us saved, sanctified, and filled with the Holy Ghost folks. Are you a Christian or a sodomite? Can a Christian operate as a sodomite? The point—a sodomite is not a person. It is, however, a spirit within a person.

We must unveil this spirit. For one thing, many homosexuals and lesbians are being delivered but not made free (or maybe I should say *made whole*). If God delivered you from the spirit of homosexuality, you can still be in a heterosexual relationship doing sodomite activities. Delivered, but not made whole. As we bring the spirit of sodomy into the light, I pray your actions and appetites change, making you emancipated. However, we need to look deeper.

Let's pull this off the homosexuals and lesbians and place it in the ballpark with us every-day *tongue-talking, Bible-toting people of God.* For we too, can have the spirit of sodomy living in us, as shown by our actions.

When the Apostle Paul wrote to the Romans, he said, "And likewise also the men, leaving the natural use of the woman burned in their lust one toward another; men with men working that which is unseemly, and receiving in themselves that recompense of their error which was met. And even as they did not like to retain God in their knowledge; God gave them over to a reprobate mind, to do those things which are not convenient." (Romans 1:27)

Note: When we move from the way God said to live, our attitudes and actions turn into lust. We lose sight of what God intended for intimate relationships, turning the act of sex into nothing more than what animals do instead. And in their case, at least they engage one another for procreation. Because of perversion, sex often becomes a selfish act rather than an act of love between a husband and wife and worshipping the Creator in the midst of it.

"For this ye know, that no whoremonger, nor unclean person, nor covetous man, who is an idolater, hath any inheritance in the kingdom of Christ and God." (Ephesians 5:5)

So far, do you see sodomy as godly or ungodly? When we use our bodies for anything other than God's intended design, we walk in disobedience. So even if sex occurs between man and woman, husband and wife, we can still act in an ungodly manner.

The human body, so complex and intricate, has many parts, and each came with a designed purpose. For the purposes of this book, let's focus on two systems—digestive and reproductive. "The digestive system includes the esophagus, intestines, gallbladder, liver, mouth, pancreas, salivary glands and stomach. These organs work together to process food and absorb nutrients and water. The reproductive system comprises fallopian tubes, ovaries, penis, prostate, seminal vesicles, testes, uterus, vagina and vas deferens. This system makes gametes and sex hormones that enable humans to produce offspring."[3]

So how does man leave the natural use of a woman? While the next few paragraphs may not include every misused body part, consider these few areas often used in ways God didn't intend.

First, God created all of us with a mouth because, frankly, we eat with it. Part of the digestive system, the mouth also allows verbal communication. Consider as well what we put in our mouths. Most foods contain a great deal of bacteria.

Let's look deeper. Among many other interesting facts about the mouth, consider this. "Saliva protects the organs within your mouth from dehydration and aids with digestion. The tongue forms the basis for phonetics practice, language repetition, and other unique movements learned via exercises. The human mouth is actually interconnected with both the nose and the eyes. The human mouth is one of the dirtiest parts of

---

[3] (Mayer 2018)

the body, second only to the genital tract, where your pee comes from, and the intestinal tract, where poop comes out."[4]

In no way can the mouth contribute to the reproductive system, never a part of it. So why, then, should we use the mouth for oral sex?

Second, misusing the anus, part of the digestive system and in no way related to the reproductive system, can have dire consequences. "The primary job of [the] anus is to regulate the discharge of waste and indigestible substances out of the body. The job of the rectum is to store the waste products in preparation for their ultimate removal out of the body. The job of the anus, on the other hand, is to serve as an opening for the elimination of feces."[5]

While I won't go into all the potential anal diseases, none of them are pretty. Some can increase the risk of anal cancer—true for both men and women. So while you may feel anal sex is okay because you're married, consider potential risks. Besides being outside of God's will, you may also inadvertently cause a great deal of pain for your loved one.

(If you want gory, detailed information, you may want to read the article found at www.ncbi.nlm.nih.gov/pmc/articles/PMC27800

---

[4] (Chan 2016)
[5] (Isaac n.d.)

56/.)

(3) The vagina receives the penis during sexual intercourse and also serves as a conduit for the menstrual flow from the uterus, which cleans the uterus when conception doesn't occur in preparation for future pregnancy. The natural use of these two body parts works beautifully. But consider the tongue from the dirty mouth used in oral sex. What bacteria do you introduce into a woman's body by this unnatural use?

The recent increase in concern over HPV (Human Papillomavirus) rose because "some of the over 100 types can cause cancer of the cervix, anus and penis. HPV lives in thin, flat cells called epithelial cells. These are found on the skin's surface. They're also found on the surface of the vagina, anus, vulva, cervix and head of the penis. They're also found inside the mouth and throat."[6] Again, we raise the question of why would we misuse the tongue and vagina during sex, knowing if we leave the natural uses, we can cause a myriad of issues.

During childbirth, the baby passes through the vagina (birth canal). We are right back in Genesis 1:28, "And God blessed them, and God said unto them, Be fruitful and multiply, and replenish the earth."

---

[6] (Web M.D. LLC, reviewed by Nvian Todd, M.D. 2019)

We know God created sexual intercourse, intending that it exist between a husband and wife for the purpose of creating children and ultimate intimacy with each other.

As long as we keep sex, whatever that looks like to us, within marriage, we are okay. Right?

Not according to God's Word and the truths He showed me during this study. Add to that the scientific evidence, which supports that God's way is in our best interest.

If we are to lie upon the marriage bed and keep it undefiled, we must do things God's way.

If we were to bring an animal into the bed, it becomes bestiality and is forbidden by God's Law. Leviticus 18:23, "Neither shalt thou lie with any beast to defile thyself therewith: neither shall any woman stand before a beast to lie down thereto: it is confusion."

Honestly, I don't understand the mindset behind this practice, but it happens. And it started long before any of us walked this earth. While most of us don't consider bringing an animal into our sexual practices, with or without a spouse, we don't hesitate to bring other practices outside of God's will into our beds. Are they any less against His will? No. He desires to bless our marriages and protect us from harm with such laws.

I know that lying down with my spouse is the will of God, whether we produce children or simply increase our intimacy. But if the spirit of sodomy appears, then we step outside of God's will.

Remember, sodomites engage in sodomy, defined as anal or oral sex between any two people or between a person and a non-human animal.

In the same way, sex outside of marriage can pervert our overall perspective on godly sex, so can dabbling around in this spirit of sodomy. Our actions regarding this matter can and will defile our marriage bed.

It's time to clean up the bed.

Chapter 5
~The Outcome from the Study~

"Better is the end of a thing than the beginning thereof: and the patient in the spirit is better than the proud in spirit."

(Ecclesiastes 7:8, KJV)

When God opens truth to us, we unlock those teachings at a risk. I felt that way when I finished studying. In ignorance, I had an excuse for the way I viewed sex. When I know truth, I can't plead innocence for ungodly behavior.

We are to stand on James 4:17, "Therefore to him that knoweth to do good, and doeth it not, to him it is sin."

So I place this question before you. After reading and studying the Word of God pertaining to sex, is sodomy a sin?

If this means we engage in sinful sexual acts, we stand guilty of performing sodomy. God considers this an unholy act, and the Word of God says, "Without holiness, no man will see God." (See Hebrews 12:14.) These sexually immoral acts make us unholy, and in doing so, we will not see God.

Does that mean we lose our salvation? No. But it does put up a barrier that interferes with the relationship God wants with us. In an ungodly state of mind and body, we honestly don't want to see God.

Remember Adam and Eve in Genesis 3. After sinning in the Garden of Eden, they hid behind the bushes after a feeble attempt at covering themselves with leaves, trying to hide their bodies. Because we know good—the right way to behave—if we chose to ignore that knowledge, we experience fear and shame. And we hide from our Creator in the same manner.

Important question. *Are we seeking the pleasures of Sodom more than we want to see God?*

Before answering, think about this. The spirit of sexual immorality crept in slowly many years ago. If we were to ask an individual (male or female) 20-30 years ago about these acts, there would have been many arguments and serious verbal and physical confrontations because they would have been offended within their moral spirit.

The tactics of the devil aren't new. We know that our fight is spiritual. "For the weapons of our warfare are not carnal, but mighty through God to the pulling down of strongholds" (2Corinthians 10:4). The city of Corinth in biblical times stank of immorality. Even within the church, sexual sin prevailed during the apostle's time. This spirit does not remain in the world undetected—it has made its way into the body of Christ, just as it did back in Paul's time.

Many will try to stand on the married bed as being undefiled after all of these scriptures and revelation from the Holy Spirit. We can use that as justification, but look closely at your walk with God. If we must justify an action, could it be we know deep inside the act is wrong? If you see any room for growth, then perhaps this one thing holds the key to an even stronger relationship with Him. I ask you to study and pray that the Holy Ghost will lead you to the will of God. According to the Word of God, in Matthew 17:21, "But this kind goes not out but by prayer and fasting."

Holiness goes far beyond a look. It is a way of life, whether in public, private or utterly alone. Holiness is defined in Hebrew as *Qa'dhesh* and conveys the thought of separateness, exclusiveness or sanctification to God, who is holy; a state of being set aside to the service of God. In the Greek scripture, the words rendered holy (ha`gios), holiness (hagiasomos), and sanctification (hagiotes; hagiosyne) likewise denote a separation to God. They also are used to refer to holiness as a quality of God and to purity or perfection in one's personal conduct.

2Corinthians 7:1 comes into play having, therefore, these promises, dearly beloved. Let us cleanse ourselves from all filthiness of the flesh and spirit, including the watching of pornography, and perfecting our holiness in the fear of God. If we are to walk holy in this world, we cannot justify actions and look like the world.

But what if the unclean spirits stop us from seeing the true motive of God—His love for us? Would you kill them? I truly know this is the will of God for my life due to the fact of how and why this is being revealed to me. I now understand those seven years I had to write letters to keep in contact with my loved ones was all in preparation for the writing of this book. Thank you, Jesus, for taking what the enemy meant for bad and turning it around for all our good.

As previously stated, there are only two types of people in this world, the good and the bad or the saved and the unsaved. Still, we all sin before and after salvation. Nevertheless, "if we confess our sins, He is faithful and just to forgive us our sins, and to cleanse us from all unrighteousness."

(1John 1:9) I pray that from this study and the reading of this book, Holy Spirit brings the body of Christ to repentance.

This spirit is not just sex-related. There is much more to this sin because it starts with heart attitudes. We must stand on the Word of God and not continue to believe in something passed down from an unlearned body of believers. We must be the generation that studies the Word of God personally and destroys those clichés that keep us in bondage.

To give you one that has no truth in it, "God destroyed Sodom and Gomorrah because of homosexuality," and that's not true. Look at Genesis 18:20 to discover the reason for him doing so, "And the Lord said, 'Because the cry of Sodom and Gomorrah is great and because their sin is very grievous.'"

This is why this unclean spirit must be removed from among us as believers. Sex is for the use of worship between husband and wife but must be done in the beauty of holiness. Since sex is a part of worship, God must receive it as righteousness. God is a spirit, and they that worship Him must worship Him in spirit and in truth. John 4:24 states that Jesus was moving worship from a place and location to the heart of His people. Our hearts must be in the right place when we come to a Holy God. The sin of sodomy brings all other types of sins and perversions into the hearts and minds of God's people. It is a must that we come to repentance of these ungodly acts and all that they bring to God's people.

2 Chronicles 7:14, "If my people, which are called by my name, shall humble themselves: and pray, and seek my face, and turn from their WICKED WAYS, then will I hear from heaven and will forgive their sin, and I will heal their land."

We can so easily point at people around us, blame today's culture, and justify our actions because of these things. Never has something been right because everyone else does it, although as kids, we often tried to convince our parents we could do something for that reason. Because we belong to God, changing the winds of our time starts with us. *It starts with me.*

I truly thank God for Deuteronomy 29:29. "The secret things belong unto the Lord our God: but those things which are revealed belong unto us and to our children forever; that we may do all the words of own will."

For years, I walked in this very same spirit, blind to its true effects. This revelation is for our children and us forever. Our sex life must be pure because it is worship to God.

Another area we must fix when it comes to sex is in the removing of birth control. I can see many of you raising eyebrows at me for this statement, but bear with me.

The Word of God asks us to be fruitful, multiply, and replenish the earth. But along with the spirit of sodomy is the spirit of fear. Fear lies in our beds, telling those who lack faith that we should not have children because of our lack. We can't afford children. In essence, that means we no longer believe God will provide life's necessities. Do we not trust His ability to give us everything needed for our children?

Addressing this, please keep two scriptures in mind. Hebrews 11:6 states, "Without faith it is impossible to please God, and Psalm 37:25 assures us, "I have been young, and now am old; yet I have not seen the righteous forsaken, nor his seed begging bread."

As we live in fear of having too little and not trusting God's provision, the ungodly continue producing children. That means the earth is being filled with ungodly human beings. If we do not contribute to the population and raise our children to honor God, who will speak of Him in the future?

Should we have a dozen children? That's between you and God. But do not let fear keep you from having children. Trust that if God allows a pregnancy, He has a plan for that child. As a parent, you must feed, clothe, house and educate. Nowhere does God say keep your child in expensive clothes and give them every gadget known to man. Nor do they need a high-end car at 16. Could it be our biggest fear isn't about necessities, but more about keeping up with the people next door?

What is God's plan? How many children does He want for your family? Forget your trepidation. Ask Him, and walk in obedience to that end.

Think back to the story of Onan, which we looked at earlier. (Geneses 38:8-10) While he disobeyed from a motive other than fear, his attitude and actions still displeased God.

While we don't necessarily "spill our seed on the ground," neither do we always let it go where intended. And if we do, doctors give us many options to keep the man's seed from implanting. Who are we to thwart God's plan? Do we believe His timing is perfect?

Now is the time for the godly men and women to stand up and be obedient to the will of God to become fruitful on the earth. We must be fruitful after our own kind, meaning the saved produce those most likely to embrace salvation, so the unsaved may have a chance to know God's salvation also.

Sex in the Kingdom must be talked about openly within the body of Christ, so the Christians teach each other what is right according to God. If we do not speak up, teach and listen as godly men and women to those who do not know, the world will. And what the world tells those in the Kingdom who do not know the truth will be very wrong and detrimental to God's Kingdom here on earth.

Chapter 6
~The Hidden Act~

"My people are destroyed for lack of knowledge: because thou hast rejected knowledge, I will also reject thee, that thou shalt be no priest to me: seeing thou hast forgotten the law of thy God, I will also forget thy children."

(Hosea 4:6, KJV)

As already stated, sex was given for the reproduction of the human race. "And God blessed them, and God said unto them, Be fruitful and multiply, and replenish the earth, and subdue it and have dominion over the fish of the sea, and over the fowl of the air, and over every living thing that moveth upon the earth." (Genesis 1:28)

Needless to say, for the married people on the earth, it is critical always to remember that once a TRUTH is established, we must never forget it.

Consider this TRUTH from Genesis 3:1. "Now the serpent was more subtle than any beast of the field which the Lord God had made." Let's add the other TRUTH from Hosea 4:6, "My people are destroyed for lack of knowledge: because thou hast rejected knowledge…."

Now, to get full understanding, let's define a word.

The word *subtle* is defined as crafty. The meaning of the word crafty means "clever at achieving one's aims by indirect or deceitful methods."

Keep these two truths in mind at all times when facing that old serpent, the devil. He is a master at deception, the father of lies. The Word of God lets us know the power of his ability to deceive.

Look at Matthew 24:24. "For there shall arise false Christs, and false prophets, and shall shew great signs and wonders; insomuch that, if it were possible, they shall deceive the very elect."

The false Christ's and false prophets are all workers of iniquity, representative or agents in the earth realm on behalf of the devil. Unfortunately, they clothe themselves to look like a representative of God. We must understand that the devil will never stop trying to trap the human race by his devices.

This book was finished, over, but I couldn't get anyone to do the book cover. I sat with people in front of their computers and gave them everything and still nothing.

While sitting at home one day, God said to me, "There are dangerous sex acts going on that I need you to expose. That old serpent is using a deceitful method over a group of people that need to see the danger of the Spirit of a sodomite. There are people in the body of Christ that are healed but not made whole."

The Spirit drew me to Luke 17:19. "And he said to him, Rise and go. Your faith has made you whole."

Dr. Terry Ellis, on July 12, 2016, stated, "But do even 10 percent of us make the connection between healing and wholeness?"

Probably not. Most people take for granted the healing that comes in an infinite variety of ways. Yet they fail to take the next step of genuine gratitude and devotion to God. Many are healed—few are made whole.

The chief purpose of grace waves is to alert you to God's grace so you can move forward with wholeness. Very few people are aware of the difference, but I want you to be one of them.

So, what about you? Are you healed? Or made

whole?

One cannot give a righteous answer until this deception is made known. To those in the body of Christ healed from homosexual and bisexual lifestyle, it is crucial to be made whole from the spirit of a sodomite once you are delivered.

The danger of sodomy, "sexual intercourse involving anal or oral copulation," has the power of holding a person in the place of healing, but far from wholeness. These acts were that of their old man, and the beliefs can't die until you do away with the spirit of sodomy. The new man doesn't have a chance to be made whole because of the old acts that continue. A man or a woman can be delivered from homosexuality, get a husband or wife, and continue those past acts.

Who are they within their mind? This setup the old serpent uses holds them in a lost state of mind. The question is, who are they truly with—their husband or wife? Or are they with former lovers of their past? As a man or woman thinks in their heart, so is he or she. God's will is for us not just to be healed, but to be made whole. The truth about the spirit of sodomy has been one of those matters kept in the dark.

Wholeness comes when we completely do away with the act of sodomy. "For this cause God gave them up unto vile affections: for even their women did change the natural use into that which is against nature." (Romans 1:26) Human nature falls under the reproduction system God gave to the human race in a marriage between a husband and wife. Genesis says Adam knew his wife. The word "knew" refers to sexual intercourse. When we manipulate the reproductive system, we go against nature.

Whenever God exposes the truth, He never intends that knowledge to bring any down, but to bring them out into His marvelous light. "'Have I any pleasure at all that the wicked should die?' saith the Lord God, 'and not that he should return from his ways, and live?'" (Ezekiel 18:23)

Now that the visor has been pulled back, how do you look in the eyesight of God? It is time to return our sex life to God, unto righteousness. We must face these serious mind battles. I pray the words written here bring someone to repentance and back to righteousness.

This is the dispensation to be made whole, knowing our Lord and Savior Jesus Christ is undoubtedly soon to come.

Changing something so deeply embedded isn't easy. If the desire to change exists, but your mind or body resists, a fast may need to take place, with much prayer, for God to wash your mind from the acts that take place there.

Paul wrote to Corinthians, who, by the way, struggled with sexual sins, and encouraged them to bring thoughts under captivity. In this age, do we need this instruction any less?

"Casting down imaginations, and every high thing that exalteth itself against the knowledge of God, and bringing into captivity every thought to the obedience of Christ." (2Corinthians 10:5)

Chapter 7
~You Took the Risk~

"Put not your trust in princes, nor in the son of man, in whom there is no help."
(Psalms 146: 3, KJV)

Now that you have taken the risk and opened this book, where do you go from here?

Sex in the Kingdom is a topic not openly discussed. The truth of God's Word in true holiness has always been here. For so long, most of us simply read His Word instead of studying it intensely. We overlooked this truth about sodomy in our God-given relationships.

Many husbands and wives have engaged in this sinful act for years, and many will fight this eye-opening truth due to fleshly appetites they enjoy in the darkness of sinful acts. Now we face sexual strongholds that are not easy to let go because of the pleasure it provides to our flesh. We must understand this old saying is so true—"Sin will take you farther than you want to go, keep you longer than you want to stay, and cost you more than you want to pay." (Ravi Zacharias)

I didn't write this book to judge nor condemn, but to bring awareness to the Kingdom of God. All sin must come to the place of repentance. In 1John 1:9 (NIV), we read, "If we confess our sins, he is faithful and just and will forgive us our sins and purify us from ALL unrighteousness."

Think back over the things considered a stronghold that you overcame. At the time, you had to go to God for help. In the fight of our spiritual life, we know going to man often yields opinions rather than God's truth.

Now is the time to pray like never before because this sexual stronghold will not just let you walk away. We are creatures of habit, good or bad. This truth can be dangerous to the relationship between a husband and wife because of the enjoyment that it gave them over the years. Let's face it, we can enjoy all manner of sinful acts, but that doesn't mean we want to keep doing them.

This is why there has to be much prayer and fasting because these types of habits are only destroyed by praying and fasting. Remember the

Word of God assures us that "whoever the Son sets free is free indeed." (John 8:36) We must let God free the other person as well as us as the release of desires will be a fight of the flesh.

I have come to understand that this request of releasing unclean spirits can be a hard place for many. But Jesus said, "If you love me; keep my commandments." (John 14:15)

This word commandment means a divine rule, and it implied keeping those rules. Many focused on the Ten Commandments when Jesus spoke these words, but He spoke of many sayings, and Jesus didn't stop with the law. He also focused on the heart attitudes. We know right and wrong, and if we listen, Holy Spirit speaks truth to our hearts. Then, we have no excuse for continuing in sin. "Therefore, to him that knoweth to do good, and doeth it not, to him it is sin." James 4:17

Sodomy is a sinful act for whoever commits the act. The idea of changing can overwhelm us, but be of good cheer. The situation isn't hopeless. The same Jesus that delivers us from all our sins is more than able to do the same for this one. Sodomy must be faced with the Word of God. Delivered people deliver others, and undelivered people keep others undelivered.

Be careful whom you ask for an opinion or help because if they haven't studied this matter in its entirety, they can only give you half of an answer. And those people may answer based on half-truths, opinions or even scripture taken out of context.

If I was going to Las Vegas, and they told me I had a 50-50 chance to win, GET OUT OF THE WAY because I'm playing all night. However, on a 50-50 chance of my soul being lost, I'll pass. I need to know 100 percent about this matter if my soul and its wellness are at stake. That's why this book has a study behind it. I absolutely understand there is more to be studied. God has someone that will come after me to add to these words. Inevitably, there is nothing new under the sun, and there is a possibility it may already exist. We are the body of Christ and must take the issue of uncleanliness to heart. As you read and study, I pray God shows you His will for your application of this book.

We must get back to Genesis 1:27-28. God created them. God blessed them, and God said unto them, "Be fruitful and multiply, and replenish the earth." That is His will for humanity—to replenish, and this can only be done the way God ordained it through a husband and wife.

Many will close their eyes to the truths presented in this book. But I have completed my task according to God's will. The "Study of the Matter" presented revelation with a foundation and principles to stand on. The truth from the study provides the body of Christ a reason to look into other facts, whether stated in this book or not. Now that some eyes are open, remember—do not take the approach of a hypocrite. "Thou hypocrite, first cast out the beam out of thine own eye; and then shalt thou see clearly to cast of the mote of thy brother's eye." (Matthew 7:5)

In closing, according to the Bible, sex was given to husbands and wives, **men and women**, to fulfill the decree God gave to mankind in Genesis 1:27-28. I pray the risk you took in opening this book pays huge dividends. AMEN.

References

Chan, Dr. Keith Andrew. 2016. "10 Disgusting Facts
        About the Human Mouth." *Listverse.* July 20.
        listverse.com/2016/07/20/10-disgusting-facts-
        about-the-human-mouth/.

Isaac, M. n.d. "ANUS DEFINITION, PARTS, DISEASES AND
        FUNCTIONS IN HUMAN DIGESTIVE SYSTEM."
        Organs of the Body. Accessed August 21, 2019.
        www.organsofthebody.com/anus/.

Mayer, Melissa. 2018. "Body Systems & Their
        Functions." *Sciencing.* July 25.
        www.sciencing.com.

Merriam-Webster Incorporated. 2019. www.merriam-
        webster.com.

Richard Broadbent, III. 2012. *The Little Red Prayer Book.*
        Lexington, KY: Christain Word Ministries.
        Accessed June 13, 2019.
        www.christianword.org.

Web M.D. LLC, reviewed by Nvian Todd, M.D. 2019.
        "Information About the Human Papillomavirus
        (HPV)." *WebMD.* April 3. www.webmd.com.

~*About the Author*~

Currently the Overseer of the SURGE Center of Dallas, Texas, Apostle Stanley J. Alexander has faithfully served there for the past four years. Formerly the Pastor of Abundantly Blessed Ministries for nine years, he lives in the Dallas area with his wife, Paula.

www.ingramcontent.com/pod-product-compliance
Lightning Source LLC
Chambersburg PA
CBHW061157040426
42445CB00013B/1710